• T R O P H I E S •

Intervention
PRACTICE BOOK
Grade 3

Harcourt

Orlando Boston Dallas Chicago San Diego

Visit *The Learning Site!*
www.harcourtschool.com

Table of Contents

Fluency Builder

department	all	bags
obeys	there	flat
commands	were	back
audience	sad	glad
expression	class	fast
accident	stamp	clap
noticed	pack	

1. Dan / looked at all the letters, / and he was sad.

2. There were letters / for Alf Sands / at the police department.

3. There were letters / for the students / in Ann Grant's class.

4. Nan / had to stamp / the letters.

5. Hank / had to pack / the letters / in bags.

6. Brad / had an accident / and fell flat / on his back.

7. Then / Dan's expression / went from sad / to glad.

8. He noticed / Fran / and asked her / to get the letters out / fast.

9. Fran obeys / Dan's commands / to get the letters / to Alf Sands / and Ann Grant's class.

10. Ann Grant's class / is so glad / that they clap and clap / for Fran. / What an audience!

Dan and Fran

Look at the pictures. Write the word from the box that best completes each sentence.

van	crab	hat	mat	jam
bag	bat	lap	sand	dam

1. Tad is in the _____van_____.

2. His dad has a _____bat_____.

3. I see Jan on a _____mat_____.

4. The cat is in her _____lap_____.

5. Pam can make a _____dam_____.

6. Nat has a _____bag_____.

7. Dan sees the _____jam_____.

8. His _____hat_____ is in his hand.

9. "Look, Jack! I see a _____crab_____!"

10. Jack ran in the _____sand_____.

Harcourt

Dan and Fran

These events are from "Dan and Fran." They are out of order. Put a number in front of each one to show the right order.

_____2_____ Dan sees Fran.

_____3_____ Fran grabs the letters.

_____1_____ Dan has many letters to send out.

_____4_____ Fran cannot make a speech, but Dan can.

Now write each event in the order it happens in the story. Put each one next to an X.

[X] Dan has many letters to send out. _____

[X] Dan sees Fran. _____

Dan asks Fran to help. _____

[X] Fran grabs the letters. _____

Fran hands out the letters to everyone. _____

Ann Grant's students clap and clap. _____

[X] Fran cannot make a speech, but Dan can. _____

_____

_____

_____

Decode Long Words

Read these long words. Draw a picture to show what each word means.

backpack

rabbit

sandbox

Harcourt

Fluency Builder

grumble	is	tricks
exploded	that	big
language	down	pink
mumbled	said	pig
streak	with	sit
stubborn	came	did
darted		twins

1. Miss Mack / is a big, / pink pig. / Kim / is teaching her to do tricks.

2. "Sit down. / Sit down." / Kim said it / twice. / She said it softly.

3. "Miss Mack / is stubborn," / said Kim / with a grumble.

4. "That's because / you mumbled," / said Nick.

5. "Are you teaching / Miss Mack / in kid language?" / asked Jill.

6. Jill said, / "Stand up!" / and Miss Mack / did.

7. "Why did / my pig / listen to you?" / Kim exploded.

8. "I / can speak / pig language," / said Jill.

9. The twins / came over / with their black cat, / Ink.

10. Miss Mack said, / "Yip!" / and Ink / darted off / like a black streak.

Miss Mack's Tricks

Fill in the oval in front of the sentence that tells about the picture.

1 ⬭ That is a big pin!
  ⬭ I see six pigs.
  ⬬ One pig sits still.

2 ⬭ Kim and Jim sit in the van.
  ⬬ Kim and Jim are twins.
  ⬭ The ship is black.

3 ⬭ The cat sits in my lap.
  ⬭ I see a pig in a tin.
  ⬬ That cat fits in the tin.

4 ⬬ The lid is in her hand.
  ⬭ Sid hid the lid.
  ⬭ Lin picks up the wig.

5 ⬭ They are sitting in a ship.
  ⬬ Tim and his dad will go on a trip.
  ⬭ Tim can see a big stick.

6 ⬭ Did he get a big hat?
  ⬭ The pin is in the tin.
  ⬬ Nick likes his pin.

Harcourt

Miss Mack's Tricks

Complete the story strip to tell about the important events in "Miss Mack's Tricks."

Who is Miss Mack? a pig _____ _____ _____	What does Kim want to teach Miss Mack? tricks _____ _____ _____	
Who can speak pig language? Jill _____ _____ _____	How does Jill teach Miss Mack? with her hands _____ _____ _____	Who is Ink? a cat _____ _____ _____
Who grabs Ink? Miss Mack _____ _____ _____	What did you like in "Miss Mack's Tricks"? Responses will vary. _____ _____ _____	

Narrative Elements

Complete the story map for "Miss Mack's Tricks."

Characters	Setting
Miss Mack, Kim, Nick, Jill, Tim, Jim, Ink	**Time:** Now **Place:** Kim's yard

Plot

Beginning: Kim wants to teach Miss Mack to do tricks.

Middle: Jill uses her hands to teach Miss Mack.

End: Miss Mack grabs Ink.

Harcourt

Fluency Builder

detective	you	Tom
specific	get	mom
positive	two	box
case	have	letterbox
returned	some	got
definitely	my	Bond
assistant		drop

1. Tom, / the detective, / tells Min, / "You / can be / my assistant."

2. Min's mom / was supposed to get / two letters.

3. Min / definitely slid two letters / into the box.

4. Tom / said, / "The letterbox is full. I think / some letters fell out."

5. Mr. Bond said / that some letters / did drop out.

6. Min asked, / "Are you positive / my missing letter / will be returned?"

7. He said, / "I have / no specific information."

8. Min said to Tom, / "I am glad / you could solve / this case for me."

Name _____

The Case of the Missing Letter

Circle and write the word that makes the sentence tell about the picture.

1. Spot likes to dig at the

_____ pond _____.

(**pond**) **pot** **pop**

2. Dot said, "It is

_____ hot _____, Spot!"

top **clock** (**hot**)

3. Spot hops over a

_____ rock _____.

(**rock**) **lock** **rod**

4. Spot looks like a

_____ mop _____!

(**mop**) **got** **lock**

5. "Spot, _____ stop _____

sock **shop** (**stop**)

that now!" said Dot.

6. Now Dot is

_____ not _____ so hot!

(**not**) **job** **plop**

Harcourt

The Case of the Missing Letter

Think about the mystery or problem in "The Case of the Missing Letter." How does Tom solve it? Write in the boxes to tell about important parts of the story.
Responses will vary.

What is the mystery?

Min mailed two letters, but her mom only got one.
The mystery is what happed to the other letter.

What clues does Tom find?

The letterbox is very full. A stamp is on the grass.

How is the case solved?

A letter without a stamp gets returned, so Tom tells Min to check
her own box.

Harcourt

Decode Long Words

Look at the words. Write the word parts in the boxes.

	short word		short word
backpack	back	+	pack

	short word		ending
painting	paint	+	ing

	short word		word part
suddenly	sudden	+	ly

	word part		short word
unable	un	+	able

Read the sentences. Use the words above to finish the sentences.

1. _____ Suddenly _____ it began to rain.

2. I am _____ painting _____ a picture.

3. Anna had her _____ backpack _____ on.

4. He is _____ unable _____ to lift the big box.

Fluency Builder

pretended	make	went
familiar	look	red
professional	when	get
captain	into	set
aimed	laugh	net
monitor	was	fell
	best	let

1. Ted / went to the playground / with his red basketball.

2. Pat / was getting set / to make a basket.

3. Ted pretended / not to look.

4. Pat's basketball / fell / into the net.

5. Ted didn't want Pat / to laugh / when his ball / missed the net.

6. Ted / looked familiar / to Pat.

7. His dad / was a professional / and a team captain.

8. Pat / helped her new friend / Ted / as he aimed the ball / at the net.

9. The playground monitor / let in / Ted's dad.

10. He / was the best teacher / for Pat.

Just a Little Practice

Read the story. Circle all the words where the letter *e* stands for the short vowel sound you hear in *bed*.

"Jen, do you want to go sledding?" asked Fred. Jen said, "Yes! Let's go!" Fred got his red sled. Jen got her black sled. Jen led Fred up the hill. They went up to the top. Fred went down fast! He sped past ten men. Jen went next. She sped past ten hens!

Jen said, "Fred, that was the best!"

Fred said, "Yes. Now I have to rest!"

Write a word that you circled in the story to complete each sentence.

1. Fred and Jen will go _____sledding_____.

2. Fred has a _____red_____ sled.

3. Jen _____led_____ Fred to the top of the hill.

4. Fred sledded past ten _____men_____.

5. Jen passed ten _____hens_____.

6. Now Fred will _____rest_____.

Harcourt

Just a Little Practice

Fill in the story map to tell about the main events in "Just a Little Practice."

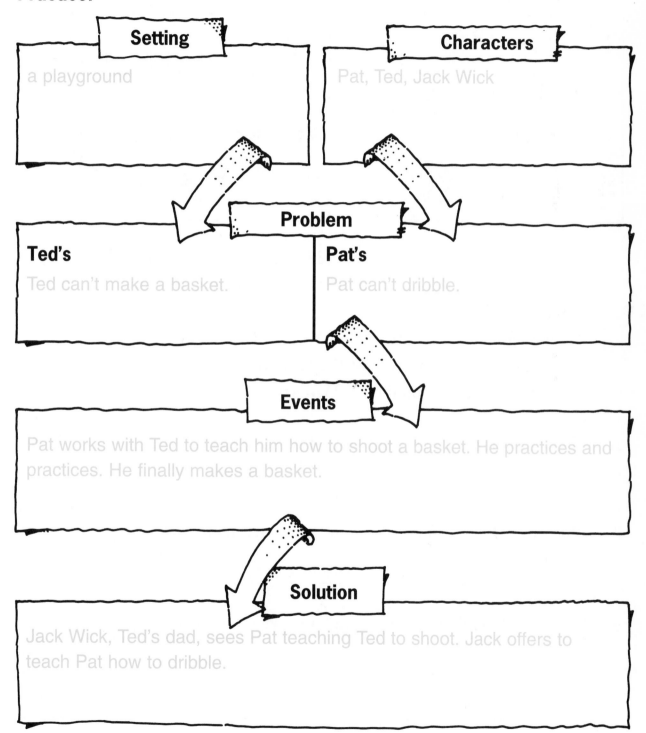

Setting

a playground

Characters

Pat, Ted, Jack Wick

Problem

Ted's

Ted can't make a basket.

Pat's

Pat can't dribble.

Events

Pat works with Ted to teach him how to shoot a basket. He practices and practices. He finally makes a basket.

Solution

Jack Wick, Ted's dad, sees Pat teaching Ted to shoot. Jack offers to teach Pat how to dribble.

Harcourt

Name _____

Narrative Elements

Read the story. Then answer the questions.

    Don is playing with his friend. He sees his mom with a big box. "Let me help you, Mom," he says. He stops playing and runs to help his mom.

    Now Don's friend Matt has lost his ball. Don helps Matt look for it. It takes hard work, but at last they find the ball.

    "Thank you for helping me," Matt says.

1. What can you tell about what kind of person Don is?

_____Possible response: He is helpful._____

2. What does Don say that helps you know what he is like?

_____"Let me help you, Mom."_____

3. What does Don do that helps you know what he is like?

_____He helps his mom and his friend._____

_____

Harcourt

Fluency Builder

ancient	with	but
compete	will	must
host	games	run
stadium	some	sun
medals	have	
record	one	
ceremonies	over	
earned	into	

1. An ancient stadium / is host / to the Olympics.

2. You parade / with the athletes / into the stadium.

3. You will not / compete today, / but you cannot / rest.

4. You must run / every day / to be fit.

5. Some athletes / have earned medals, / and one / has set a record.

6. The sun / is going down, / and you / must get to bed.

7. In the stadium, / you get set / and listen / for the gun / that tells you to run.

8. When the games / are over, / the medal ceremonies / will be held.

You Are in the Olympics

Read the sentences. Then follow the directions.

1. Make the bug on the mug red.

2. Make nuts to go in the dish.

3. Find the jug. Draw a cup to go with the jug.

4. Who is scrubbing? Make him stand on a rug.

5. Who is cutting? Make plums for her to cut.

6. Give the pup a bun.

Harcourt

Name _____

You Are in the Olympics

Complete the flowchart with words from the box to tell about "You Are in the Olympics."

bus	bed	win	running

The girl is here for the

___running___

competitions.

→

When the sun goes

down, she must go to

___bed___.

The athletes go to the

stadium in a

___bus___.

→

The girl starts off well,

but does she

___win___?

Answer these questions to tell about the rest of the story.

1. Who wins the running competition? _____ the girl _____

_____

2. What does the girl get at the medal ceremonies? _____ a gold medal _____

_____

3. What can the girl do now? _____ She can just have fun. _____

_____

Elements of Nonfiction

Write words from the box to tell about the nonfiction books and articles.

informational book	**biography**	**newspaper article**
	how-to article	

biography

how-to article

newspaper article

informational book

Harcourt

Fluency Builder

eager	tells	then
litter	me	now
patiently	but	what
trained	find	when
wise	down	with
message	gives	bath
	could	things

1. Mom says / the beach has / a secret, / and I am eager / to see / what it is.

2. Mom tells me / we can't dig, / but we can / collect litter.

3. I find / lots of weird things, / but I do not find / the secret.

4. When we run / down to the beach, / there are fishing ships / dancing / on the sea.

5. I get up / on a big rock / with Mom, / and we sit / patiently.

6. Then / I see the turtles / run down the beach / to the rocks, / and the sea / gives them / a bath.

7. It looks as if / they have trained / to run that fast.

8. "What / are they / going to do / now?" / I ask.

9. "That / is the secret / of the wise sea," / Mom says.

10. I wish / I could get / a message / to the turtles.

Harcourt

Name_____

The Race to the Sea

Fill in the oval in front of the sentence that tells about the picture.

1 ● The dog gets a whiff.
○ The dog gets a bath.
○ The dog gets to run on the path.

2 ○ Miss Smith finds a moth.
● Miss Smith sees a path.
○ Miss Smith is doing math.

3 ○ "What a thick jar!" he said.
○ "You have a thin dish," he said.
● "The thin one is for me," he said.

4 ○ The dog sits in the path.
○ The dog sees the moth.
● The dog has a bath.

5 ○ Stan sits on a thick log.
● Stan whips up a thick broth.
○ Stan has a thick cloth.

6 ● Seth thinks to do his math.
○ Seth has to make a moth.
○ Seth sees something in the bath.

The Race to the Sea

Complete the puzzle using words from the box.

secret	tomorrow	sea	rock	weird	beach

Across

3. He sees turtles digging on the _____.

5. They run fast into the _____.

6. The sun sets, so he will have to go back to the beach _____.

Down

1. The boy gets up on a _____ and looks for the secret.

2. Mom said the beach has a _____.

4. Turtles look _____ with sand on them.

Write the completed sentences in the order in which they happened in the story.

Mom said the beach has a secret.

The boy gets up on a rock and looks for the secret.

The sun sets, so he will have to go back to the beach tomorrow.

He sees turtles digging on the beach.

Turtles look weird with sand on them.

They run fast into the sea.

Harcourt

Author's Purpose

Read about each book. Write the author's purpose to complete the sentence.

1. This book tells how to take care of your pet cat. It tells facts about cats.

The author's purpose is

_____to inform_____.

2. This book tells why the author thinks children should read more.

The author's purpose is

_____to persuade_____.

3. This book tells a story about a frog who gets a new hat.

The author's purpose is

_____to entertain_____.

Harcourt

Fluency Builder

telegraph	come	Hatch
drifts	know	ranch
temperature	went	Patches
guided	find	inch
trail	someone	Champ
splinters	along	watches
	first	
	that	

1. Frank Hatch / is out hunting / with Brandon Hatch, / who is 12.

2. The temperature drops, / and a bad snowstorm / starts.

3. The wind / makes the snow hit hard, / like splinters of ice.

4. Mrs. Hatch / watches, / but she can't / telegraph / Frank and Brandon / to come back.

5. She doesn't know / if they went north / or south / from the ranch.

6. Champ and Patches / are dogs / that can find / someone who is lost.

7. First, / the dogs / sniff something / that belongs to Frank / or Brandon.

8. Then, / they sniff / along the trail, / hunting / for that smell.

9. The dogs / inch along / in the drifts of snow, / but they do not stop.

10. The dogs / have guided friends / to Frank and Brandon.

Help on the Trail

Read each direction line. Then do what it tells you to do.

1. Find a chimp. Make it red.
2. Find two chicks. Make an X on them.
3. Find a chest. Make the chest black.
4. Find the big branch. Make a check on it.
5. Find a watch. Write 1, 3, 6, and 12 on it. Make the strap red.

Harcourt

Name _____

Help on the Trail

Fill in the story map to tell about the main events in "Help on the Trail."

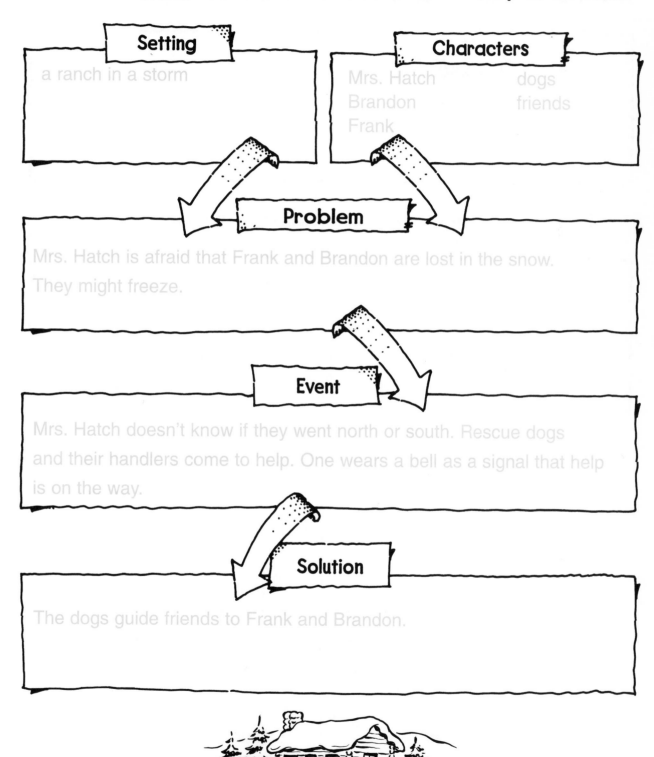

Setting

a ranch in a storm

Characters

Mrs. Hatch   dogs
Brandon   friends
Frank

Problem

Mrs. Hatch is afraid that Frank and Brandon are lost in the snow. They might freeze.

Event

Mrs. Hatch doesn't know if they went north or south. Rescue dogs and their handlers come to help. One wears a bell as a signal that help is on the way.

Solution

The dogs guide friends to Frank and Brandon.

Harcourt

Word Relationships

1. Circle the synonym. Draw a picture to show the meaning.

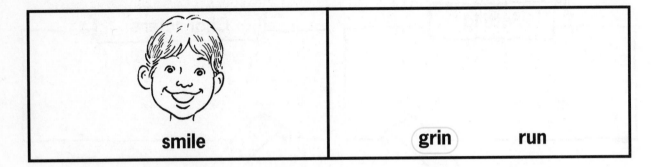

smile   grin   run

2. Circle the antonym. Draw a picture to show the meaning.

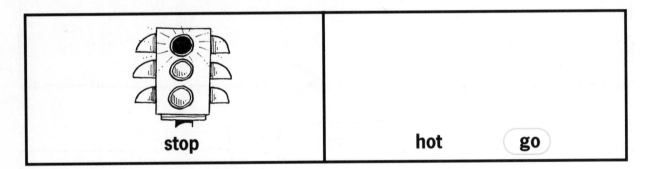

stop   hot   go

3. Circle each homophone. Draw pictures to show the meanings.

too	top two

for	four fox

Harcourt

Fluency Builder

creature	all	far
curious	watch	dark
marine	some	yard
delicate	how	park
collapsed	because	smart
survived	many	apart
		harm
		hard

1. All children / like to watch / creatures.

2. Some adults / snap photos / that let us see / how creatures survive.

3. A sub / goes far down / in the sea / to get a shot / of the marine creatures.

4. Fish, / crabs, / and delicate creatures / like / the dark sea bottom.

5. Are you curious / about the bugs / in the yard / and in the park?

6. In one shot, / a smart bug / looks like / an ant.

7. Friends with feathers / can not / tell the two apart.

8. They / do not harm / the bug / because / they don't like / an ant / for a snack.

9. In one photo, / a dad bug / with many eggs / on its back / has not collapsed.

10. It can be / hard / to be / a bug.

Creature Clicks

Read each sentence. Then follow the directions.

1. Mark an X on the parked car.

2. Make the barn red.

3. It is dark. Add stars.

4. Add grass in the yard.

5. Add rocks to the cart.

6. Carp are fish. Add carp to the pond.

Harcourt

Creature Clicks

Complete the puzzle with words from "Creature Clicks."

watch	photos	feathers	shot	notice	eggs	hatch

Across

2. Some friends with _____ will not have ants for a snack.

5. Some mom bugs sit next to the eggs until the eggs _____.

6. Everyone likes to _____ creatures.

7. The dad bug has all the _____ stuck to his back.

Down

1. Did you _____ all the bugs in the backyard?

3. It can be hard to get a _____ of some creatures.

4. Some adults get _____ of creatures.

Write two sentences about the animals in "Creature Clicks." Use some of the words from the box.

Responses will vary.

_____

_____

_____

_____

Author's Purpose

Read the lines from each selection. Write answers to the questions.

A. **Many different creatures may be found in one little pond. Fish, frogs, turtles, and bugs are just some of the creatures you might see in or near a pond.**

1. Is this selection fiction or nonfiction?

_____ nonfiction _____

2. What topic does the author tell about?

_____ creatures found in and around a pond _____

3. Is the author's main purpose to entertain, to inform, or to persuade?

_____ to inform _____

B. **Fred Frog sat in the pond. He did not want to swim. He did not want to play. The other pond creatures were curious. Why was Fred so sad?**

4. Is this selection fiction or nonfiction?

_____ fiction _____

5. Does it tell about real people and events or ones that are made up?

_____ ones that are made up _____

6. Is the author's main purpose to entertain, to inform, or to persuade?

_____ to entertain _____

Harcourt

Fluency Builder

brunch	two	storms
omelet	like	horses
peaceful	wanted	corn
erupting	when	store
lava	they	poured
escape	snort	short
	roar	more

1. There was / a snort / and then / two roars.

2. Morris Thor / had trapped / two dinosaurs.

3. One roar / was like storms / storming.

4. One roar / was like lava / erupting.

5. The short dinosaur / was as big / as two horses.

6. Morris wanted / the dinosaurs / to be pets.

7. "What if / they escape?" / said Doris. / "They are not / peaceful."

8. Morris went to the store. / When he / came back, / he mixed eggs / and poured them / in a pan.

9. For brunch, / Morris made / an omelet / and two corn muffins.

10. "Mmm," / the short dinosaur said. / "More!"

Harcourt

The Dinosaurs' Brunch

Follow each direction to write a word.

1. Write *store*. __ __ __ __ __   s t o r e

2. Change the *e* to *k*. __ __ __ __ __   s t o r k

3. Make the *st* an *f*. __ __ __ __   f o r k

4. Take off the *k*. __ __ __   f o r

5. Add a *u* after the *o*. __ __ __ __   f o u r

6. Make the *f* into a *y*. __ __ __ __   y o u r

Use the words above in sentences. Use at least two of the words in each sentence.

Responses will vary.

_____

_____

_____

_____

_____

_____

Harcourt

The Dinosaurs' Brunch

Use words from the dinosaur to complete the puzzle.

Across

1. The trap was _____ with dinosaurs in it.

4. The _____ said, "MORE!"

5. Morris went to the store to get _____.

Down

2. Morris said, "This is not _____."

3. Morris _____ two dinosaurs.

6. Doris yelled and ran for _____.

Word bank on dinosaur: crowded, dinosaur, eggs, trapped, safety, enough

Write the completed sentences in the order in which they happened.

Morris trapped two dinosaurs.

The trap was crowded with dinosaurs in it.

Doris yelled and ran for safety.

Morris went to the store to get eggs.

Morris said, "This is not enough."

The dinosaur said, "MORE!"

Harcourt

Word Relationships

Read each sentence. Write a word from the sentence in the blank.

1. Basketball is a good game, but tennis is a good sport, too.

A synonym for *game* is _____sport_____.

2. This pan is full, but the other one is empty.

An antonym for *empty* is _____full_____.

3. I will add some numbers and write the sum.

The word *sum* sounds like the word _____some_____.

4. I can't play ball today because I am acting in a play.

The word _____play_____ has two different meanings.

Draw pictures to show the two different meanings.

Harcourt

Fluency Builder

program	who	she
comfortable	he	Flash
appointment	one	shops
approach	will	wish
firm	help	Sharon
confident	said	rushed
equipment	named	

1. My sister Sharon / is part of / a special program.

2. She / is training / a gentle pup / named Flash / to be / a working dog.

3. One day / Flash / will use his skills / to help someone / who can't see.

4. Flash / will have to be / comfortable / about / going anywhere.

5. He / will go to / appointments, / to shops, / and to work.

6. Sharon / will train Flash / to be still / when someone / approaches him.

7. She / will be firm / and confident / when she tells Flash / what to do.

8. One day, / the kids at my school / jumped off / the playground equipment / and rushed over / to see Flash.

9. Flash let / all of them / pet him, / so I said, / "Good dog."

10. I wish that / some day / I will / be able / to train a pup / that will bring cheer / and help / to others.

A Special Pup

Read each sentence. Then follow the directions.

1. Find a fish that splashes. Make the fish red.
2. Find the fish that is not splashing. Make that fish black.
3. Find two shells. Make an X on the shells.
4. Find the big dish. Draw a red ship on it.
5. Trish wishes she had a fish. Draw a bag with a fish in it for Trish.

Harcourt

Name _____

A Special Pup

Answer the questions to tell about Flash. Possible responses are given.

1. Why is Sharon training Flash? She is training him so he can be a
working dog that helps someone who can't see.

_____

2. What makes Flash a good working dog? He is gentle, and he is smart.

_____

_____

3. Why will Sharon have to give Flash up? Once he is trained, Flash will live
with the person he is helping.

_____

4. What new places does Flash go to? He goes to work, shops, parks, and
appointments, on bus and plane trips, and to school.

_____

5. What will be one of the best parts of training Flash? taking him on a
plane trip

_____

6. Why does the boy say "Good dog" to Flash at school? Flash lets all the
kids pet him; he is doing a good job.

_____

Harcourt

Decode Long Words

**Look at each word. Write the word parts in the boxes.
Then read the word.**

extended	ex	tend	ed
magnetic	mag	net	ic
handlebar	hand	le	bar
refreshments	re	fresh	ments

Read each sentence. Does the underlined word make sense in the sentence?

1. We had <u>refreshments</u> at the party.

2. The <u>magnetic</u> toy stuck to the metal.

3. The <u>handlebar</u> on my bike got bent.

4. The ladder <u>extended</u> to the top of the house.

Harcourt

Fluency Builder

cartwheel	my	playground
seriously	new	town
mustache	some	unwound
fastened	went	frowned
beyond	how	about
collection	around	brown
	down	outstanding

1. Rick's car / and the moving van / went down the block / around the playground/, and beyond it.

2. "Rick was / my best friend," / Howard said seriously / to his friend Beth.

3. Rick / was moving / to a new town.

4. Howard / held Beth's kite / as she unwound some string / and fastened it / to the kite.

5. "You can get / a new best friend," / said Beth. / Howard frowned.

6. "How about / Norman?" / Beth said. / "His dad / has a brown mustache."

7. "My dog, / Bow Wow, / does not like Norman," / said Howard.

8. Norman had / a collection / of cats.

9. Beth / sank the basketball / and then / she did a cartwheel.

10. "Outstanding!" / said Howard.

Name _____

A New Best Friend

Fill in the oval in front of the sentence that tells about the picture.

1 ◯ The clown is frowning.
◯ The clown is sitting down.
⬭ The clown is going out now.

2 ⬭ The hound sniffs the ground.
◯ A clown found the hound.
◯ My hand is on the ground.

3 ◯ She found the shower.
◯ She found the floor.
⬭ She found a flower.

4 ◯ They are going downtown.
◯ They see dark clouds.
◯ They are looking at brown cows.

5 ⬭ Bill counts the cows.
◯ Bill finds cows in a cart.
◯ Bill rides on the cows.

6 ◯ A horse is on the couch.
◯ I play catch in the house.
⬭ A couch is in the house.

7 ◯ The clown sees the crowd.
◯ The clown has a flower.
⬭ The clown has found a crown.

Harcourt

A New Best Friend

Complete the flowchart with words from the box to tell what happened in "A New Best Friend."

kite	teased	string
girl	moving van	wish

Howard felt sad when he saw the _____moving van_____ take all of Rick's things away.

Howard said, "I _____wish_____ I could go, too."

Howard helped Beth fix her _____kite_____.

Howard held it and Beth added the _____string_____.

Beth _____teased_____ Howard by saying she had a secret gift for basketball.

Beth was a _____girl_____, and she was Howard's new best friend.

Answer these questions to tell about the rest of the story.

1. What does Beth tell Howard to find?

a new best friend

2. How does Beth try to help Howard get a new best friend?

by naming boys she knows

3. Why does Howard want Beth to be his new best friend?

Possible response: They like to do a lot of the same things.

Sequence

These sentences are not in time order.

Next, Bob and Art played in the park.

At last, Bob Bear had a friend.

First, Bob Bear wanted a friend.

Then he met Art Ant.

Write the sentences in the correct order to complete the diagram.

First, Bob Bear wanted a friend.

↓

Then he met Art Ant.

↓

Next, Bob and Art played in the park.

↓

At last, Bob Bear had a friend.

Harcourt

Fluency Builder

gym	for	Kirsten
perform	who	her
prefer	could	twirled
recite	found	lantern
enjoying	there	pattern
billions	their	turn
roam	make	

1. Kirsten was / not enjoying / Stars class.

2. It was not / for campers like Kirsten, / who prefer / watching the stars.

3. All the campers / were going to perform / in a talent show. / They wanted / to be stars.

4. Kirsten could see / Karen and Robert / recite their lines / from a play.

5. Jennifer twirled / in her costume.

6. Kirsten roamed / around the camp.

7. Then / she went back / to her cabin / to get / her gym bag.

8. Kirsten / found her star chart / and her lantern.

9. "There are / billions of stars / that make different patterns," / she said to Gilbert.

10. Kirsten knew / what to do / for their turn / in the talent show.

Star Time

Read the sentences, and circle the words that have the /ûr/ sound. Then follow the directions.

1. Do you see the park person? Put a P on her shirt.

2. Put two rocks in the dirt.

3. The bird wants to rest. Add another branch on the tree for the bird.

4. Circle the animal with fur.

5. Where is the turtle? Put an X on the turtle.

6. Find the log. Put a girl on the log. Draw curls on her head.

Harcourt

Star Time

Fill in the story map to tell about "Star Time." You may use the words in the gray boxes to help you.

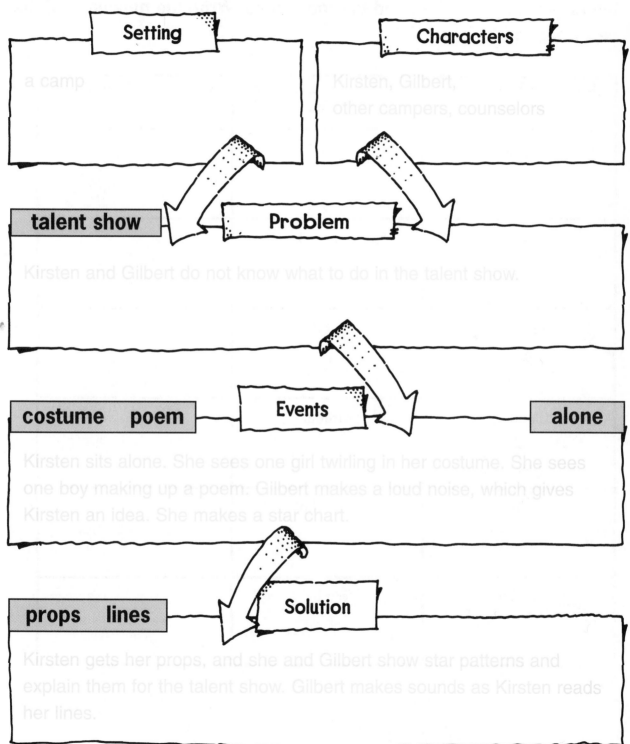

Setting

a camp

Characters

Kirsten, Gilbert, other campers, counselors

talent show

Problem

Kirsten and Gilbert do not know what to do in the talent show.

costume   poem

Events

alone

Kirsten sits alone. She sees one girl twirling in her costume. She sees one boy making up a poem. Gilbert makes a loud noise, which gives Kirsten an idea. She makes a star chart.

props   lines

Solution

Kirsten gets her props, and she and Gilbert show star patterns and explain them for the talent show. Gilbert makes sounds as Kirsten reads her lines.

Prefixes and Suffixes

Look at the new words in the first column. Think about the meanings of the prefixes and suffixes and the root words. Write the meanings of the new words in the chart.

Root Word with Prefix or Suffix	Meaning of Prefix or Suffix	Meaning of New Word
biplane	"two"	"plane with two sets of wings"
distrust	"not" or "lack of"	lack of trust
incorrect	"not"	not correct
cloudless	"without"	without clouds
painter	"one who"	one who paints
fixable	"can be"	can be fixed

Harcourt

Fluency Builder

ballhawk	game	could
vanish	were	would
fault	two	alone
depend	that	hoped
concentrate	may	dove
outfielder	look	stole
	wanted	home

1. The score / of the game / was Tans 3, / Reds 2, / and there were / two outs.

2. Jeff, / the pitcher, / was thinking / that the Reds / may bunt.

3. "They can see / I'm no ballhawk," / Jeff said.

4. "You're not alone. / Depend on Tim / and me / to look out / for bunts," / Ben said.

5. They wanted Jeff / to concentrate / on pitching.

6. Jeff hoped / Ben could catch / the pop-up fly, / but Ben couldn't, / and the Reds / scored a run.

7. "That missed catch / was my fault," / Ben said.

8. The next time, / Ben dove / for the ball / and came up with it.

9. When the Tans / got up to bat, / Tim / got a hit / and stole a base.

10. Then / Jeff hit a ball / that would vanish / over the Reds' outfielder / for a home run.

Coach Ben

Write the word that answers each riddle.

1. You can find me on the ground. I have the long *o* sound. What am I?

_____stone_____

rock   stone   penny

2. I am something you can put on. What am I?

_____robe_____

rob   rub   robe

3. I am something you can write. What am I?

_____note_____

nut   note   not

4. You can do this on one leg. What is it?

_____hop_____

hope   hop   hip

5. You can use me to get things wet. _____hose_____

house   hose   hint

6. You can tell me. What am I?

_____joke_____

jet   jack   joke

7. You can smell me. I have the long *o* sound.

What am I? _____rose_____

rose   flower   tone

Harcourt

Coach Ben

Complete the puzzle by using words from the box.

plate	hit	home run	catch	tie	score

Across

1. Tim gets a ___ in the last inning.

4. The Reds ___ two runs and are up by one run.

6. Tim steps out from in back of home ___ and goes to Jeff.

Down

2. Jeff hits a ___, and the Tans win.

3. Jeff thinks the Reds will want to bunt and ___ the game.

5. Ben cannot ___ the ball, so the Reds get two runs.

(Crossword grid with answers: 1. across/2. down "hit", "home", etc. 4. "score", 6. "plate", "catch", "run", "tie")

Write the completed sentences in the order that matches the story.

Tim steps out from in back of home plate and goes to Jeff.

Jeff thinks the Reds will want to bunt and tie the game.

Ben cannot catch the ball, so the Reds get two runs.

The Reds score two runs and are up by one run.

Tim gets a hit in the last inning.

Jeff hits a home run, and the Tans win.

Harcourt

Sequence

Read the sentences below. Write the sentences in time order in the chart.

Nat got on his bike. He picked up his cap. Finally, Nat rode home.
As he rode away, his cap fell off.

1. Nat got on his bike.

2. As he rode away, his cap fell off.

3. He picked up his cap.

4. Finally, Nat rode home.

Harcourt

Fluency Builder

glanced	coming	Mike
comfort	just	Ike
longed	right	smiled
contagious	over	size
prescription	left	griped
attention	good	time
unexpected		tried

1. Mike woke up / and smiled / because his Grandpa Ike / was coming.

2. Mom said / that Grandpa Ike / was going to share / Mike's room.

3. This news / was unexpected.

4. "My room / is just the right size / for me," / griped Mike.

5. Mike's mom / glanced over at Mike / and said / that a family shares.

6. Mike / longed for / the comfort / of a room for himself, / but he said, / "OK, Mom."

7. Mom / left for work, / where she fills prescriptions.

8. Grandpa Ike / said he and Mike / would have a good time, / and Mike tried.

9. When Mike's baby sisters / wanted more attention, / Grandpa Ike said / it was time / for just Mike.

10. Grandpa Ike's / good cheer / was contagious.

Room to Share

Follow the directions to make a word.
Then use that word in a sentence. Sentences will vary.

1. Start with *kit*. Add an *e*. What word do you get? _____ kite

_____

2. Start with *trees*. Make the first *e* an *i*. What word do you get? _____ tries

_____

3. Start with *pig*. Make the *g* an *e*. What word do you get? _____ pie

_____

4. Start with *dim*. Add an *e*. What word do you get? _____ dime

_____

5. Start with *hid*. Add an *e*. What word do you get? _____ hide

_____

6. Start with *bit*. Add an *e*. What word do you get? _____ bite

_____

Harcourt

Room to Share

Write what happened in the story. In each answer, use the words from the box.

room	tiny

Beginning: What bad news does Mike's mom give him?

Possible response: He will have to share his tiny room

with Grandpa Ike.

baby	sisters

What does Mike like about his room?

Possible response: It is the only place where he can get

away from his baby sisters.

tent	story

Middle: What are two things Grandpa Ike does with Mike?

1. Possible response: He makes a tent in Mike's room.

2. Possible response: He tells a story about Mike's mom.

family	share

End: What does Mike learn?

Possible response: It is fun to share his room with someone

in his family.

Harcourt

Prefixes and Suffixes

Prefix	Meaning
un-	"not"
dis-	"not" or "opposite of"

Suffix	Meaning
-ful	"full of"
-less	"without"

Use the meanings of prefixes and suffixes to read new words.

1. Put an X on the one that is <u>uncapped</u>.

2. Put an X on the dog that <u>disobeys</u>.

3. Make this flag <u>colorful</u>.

4. Let this flag be <u>colorless</u>.

Fluency Builder

generation   came   plate
persistently   horse   gate
illuminated   little   amazed
summoned   good   shake
faithful   inside   mane
fortunate   down   mistakes
     forgave
     lane

1. A man / had a horse / and a dog.

2. The faithful little dog / lived in the house, / and her food / came from / his plate.

3. The horse, / who lived in the barn, / ate grass / and roamed / inside the gate.

4. Yet / the lazy horse / did not recognize / his good luck.

5. Before sunrise, / a lamp / illuminated / the kitchen.

6. The horse / was amazed / to see the dog / inside.

7. That fortunate dog! / Generations of horses / had helped the man / persistently.

8. With a shake / of his mane, / the horse / stormed off / the porch.

9. The horse / made lots of mistakes, / but the man / forgave him.

10. The man / summoned the horse / to pull the cart / down the lane.

Harcourt

The Lazy Horse

Read the story, and circle all the words that have the same vowel sound you hear in *game*.

Jane and her dog sit in the shade by the lake. Jane has grapes

for a snack. She has a plate of cupcakes that she baked, too. Her

dog, Kate, wants a cupcake. Will Kate take one?

Ducks are swimming in the lake. Kate wants to chase them!

Write the word you circled in the story that best completes each sentence.

1. The girl's name is _____.

2. The dog's name is _____.

3. There is no sun in the _____.

4. Cupcakes have to be _____.

5. Kate may _____ a cupcake.

6. Kate wants to _____ some ducks.

Harcourt

The Lazy Horse

Use words from the box to complete the puzzle.

pride	chores	content	dog	house	cart

1.
p
2. c h o r e s
r
i
6. d o g
c
3.
4. h o u s e
n
t
e
n
5. c a r t

Across

2. The lazy horse did not do any _____.

3. The horse tried to behave like the _____.

4. The faithful dog lived in the _____.

5. The horse pulled the _____.

Down

1. The horse's _____ was hurt.

6. The horse learned to be _____ with himself.

Write the completed sentences in the correct story order.

Story Events from "The Lazy Horse"

The faithful dog lived in the house.

The lazy horse did not do any chores.

The horse's pride was hurt.

The horse tried to behave like the dog.

The horse pulled the cart.

The horse learned to be content with himself.

Narrative Elements

Look at the story. Tell the setting, character, problem, and solution.

MORAL: A good idea can save your life. Possible responses shown.

1. Setting: _____ outside in the hot sun _____.

2. Character: _____ a thirsty bird _____.

3. Problem: _____ The bird needs a drink _____.

4. Solution: _____ The bird drops pebbles in the water until it can get a drink. _____.

Harcourt

Fluency Builder

colonel	family	Rube
soldier	friend	recruit
brambles	through	new
weary	their	clues
outstretched	made	true
stumbling	when	flute
urgent		

1. Tom Andrews / left his family / and his home / in Blue Spring / to become / a soldier.

2. Tom's true friend / Rube Jones / was also / a recruit.

3. They trained / with other new soldiers / by going on hikes / that made them weary.

4. They listened / for clues / in the commands / of their colonel.

5. Their first job was / to take new supplies / to some soldiers / who had used / all of their own.

6. The soldiers sang / a marching song, / and Rube / played the tune / on his flute.

7. Tom and Rube / had to / take an urgent message / back to camp.

8. Stumbling through the brambles, / Tom fell / and twisted his leg, / so Rube / went on alone.

9. When Rube / came back, / Tom met him / with outstretched arms.

Harcourt

Name _____

The Bravest Soldier

Fill in the oval in front of the sentence that best tells about the picture.

1 ◯ Sue drew a tube.
⬭ Sue threw a ball.
⬤ Sue drew a fruit.

2 ◯ Chan's suit is dark.
⬤ Chan has a black suitcase.
◯ Chan sat on a suitcase.

3 ◯ June and Sam tune a flute.
◯ June's flute is blue.
⬤ Sam likes June's tune.

4 ⬤ Jim is making stew for the crew.
◯ Jim is eating fruit with the crew.
◯ Jim is staying with his crew.

5 ◯ Nick threw the ball into the basket.
◯ Nick had three blue basketballs.
⬤ Nick threw the ball to Sue.

6 ◯ Gus puts a ruler by the car.
◯ Gus puts glue on the ruler.
⬤ Gus uses glue to make a car.

The Bravest Soldier

Answer the questions to write about the story.

Beginning:

Why do Tom and Rube leave their home in Blue Spring?

_____ They are going off to be soldiers. _____

_____

Middle:

What is the first job Tom and Rube do?

_____ They take supplies to a camp. _____

_____

What special job does the colonel ask Tom and Rube to do?

_____ He asks Tom and Rube to take a message that a _____

_____ doctor is needed. _____

Ending:

Who turns out to be "the bravest soldier" and why?

_____ Rube, because he takes the message by himself when Tom gets hurt, _____

_____ and he brings back a doctor. _____

Summarize

Read the story. Write a summary that tells the important information.

Dan and Carlos took Dan's new puppy, Rex, to the park. First Rex barked at the ducks on the pond. The ducks did not seem to mind. Then Rex tried to eat the food that people were feeding the birds. The birds did not seem to mind, but the people did.

Next, Rex saw two children playing with a ball. He wanted to play, too. He jumped up and pulled the leash right out of Dan's hands. Dan and Carlos chased him all around. At last they got him and gave the ball back to the children.

Dan said, "Rex will have to learn some lessons before we bring him to the park again!"

SUMMARY

Possible response: Rex the puppy does not behave when

Dan and Carlos take him to the park. Dan won't bring him

back until he has learned to behave.

Harcourt

Fluency Builder

canyon	ago	three
gazing	inside	mean
skillful	away	creature
arranged	found	each
swiftly	things	see
pride	pictures	
feast	animals	
	over	

1. Many moons ago, / it was dark / all the time.

2. The sun, / the moon, / and the stars / were hidden / in three bags.

3. The bags / hung / inside / a mean man's house.

4. Raven was / a skillful creature / and could go / as swiftly / as an arrow / over the land.

5. Gazing down, / he could see / things happen / from miles away.

6. The mean man's wife / found a baby, / who was really Raven, / and she made / a feast.

7. The man / gave Raven / one bag / each time Raven said, / "Gah! Gah! Gah!"

8. The stars / went up / and arranged themselves / into pictures / of animals.

9. The moon / rose / over the canyon, / and out / came the sun.

10. The clever Raven / shed his costume / and shouted with pride.

Many Moons Ago

Circle and write the word that makes the sentence tell about the picture.

1. Jean walks to the

_____stream_____ .

steep   **storm**   **(stream)**

2. She likes to sit next to the tall

_____tree_____ .

(tree)   **tent**   **team**

3. The heat from the sun makes Jean

_____sleep_____ .

seam   **step**   **(sleep)**

4. Jean has a

_____dream_____ .

(dream)   **deep**   **dent**

5. In it, she sees some

_____sheep_____ .

ship   **(sheep)**   **shell**

6. Some of them are

_____eating_____ .

sleeping   **(eating)**   **leaping**

7. A _____leaf_____

lake   **leek**   **(leaf)**

wakes her up.

8. Jean says, "That was

_____neat_____ !"

need   **(neat)**   **net**

Harcourt

Many Moons Ago

Use words from the box to complete the puzzle.

pictures	stars	moon	arrow	clever	sound

Across

4. The stars form _____ of animals.

5. Raven lets the sun and the _____ out of their bags.

6. Raven goes as swiftly as an _____ to the man's home.

Down

1. Raven lets the _____ out of the bag they are in.

2. Raven is _____, and he has a plan.

3. Raven makes a _____ so the wife can find him.

Write the completed sentences in the order that matches the story.

Raven is clever, and he has a plan.

Raven goes as swiftly as an arrow to the man's home.

Raven makes a sound so the wife can find him.

Raven lets the stars out of the bag they are in.

The stars form pictures of animals.

Raven lets the sun and the moon out of their bags.

Harcourt

Compare and Contrast

Read the questions. Use words from the box to fill in the blanks in the sentences.

Raven in "Many Moons Ago"   **Real Bird**

loud	tricks	flies	beak

1. How is Raven in "Many Moons Ago" like a real bird?

He _____ flies _____ like a real bird.

He makes _____ loud _____ sounds.

He has a _____ beak _____ like a real bird.

2. How is Raven not like a real bird?

He plays _____ tricks _____ .

Harcourt

Fluency Builder

nonsense	rabbit	animals
mischief	snake	rain
duty	turtle	plains
council	food	hay
satisfied	secret	gray
tidbit	believe	tail
	king	say

1. One year, / no rain / came / to the plains, / and the animals / had no hay / to eat.

2. They called / a council meeting, / at which there was / no nonsense.

3. Gray Rabbit, / Long-Tail Snake, / and Grandpa Turtle / would lead / the animals / and keep them / from mischief.

4. They hoped / to find / even / the smallest tidbit / of food.

5. All the animals / were satisfied / with this plan.

6. The animals / found a tree / that had good things / to eat, / but the tree / had a secret.

7. Grandpa said, / "I believe it is the / king's duty / to tell us / this secret."

8. Gray Rabbit, / Long-Tail Snake, / and Grandpa Turtle / went to see / what the king / had to say.

Grandpa Tells Why

Write the word that answers each riddle.

1. You can see me on a dog. What am I? _____

tail

tall   tail   tame

2. You can ride on me. I have the same vowel sound as *gate*.

What am I? _____

train

horse   may   train

3. There are seven of me in one week.

What am I? _____

day

day   dad   dame

4. I am a color. I have the same vowel sound as *chain*.

What am I? _____

gray

gray   black   main

5. You can follow me through the woods. I have the same vowel

sound as *play*. What am I? _____

trail

path   trail   say

6. Horses eat me.

What am I? _____

hay

hail   hand   hay

7. I am something you tell a dog to do. I have the same vowel sound

as *game*. What am I? _____

stay

sit   stay   sail

Grandpa Tells Why

Fill in the story map to tell about the main events in "Grandpa Tells Why."

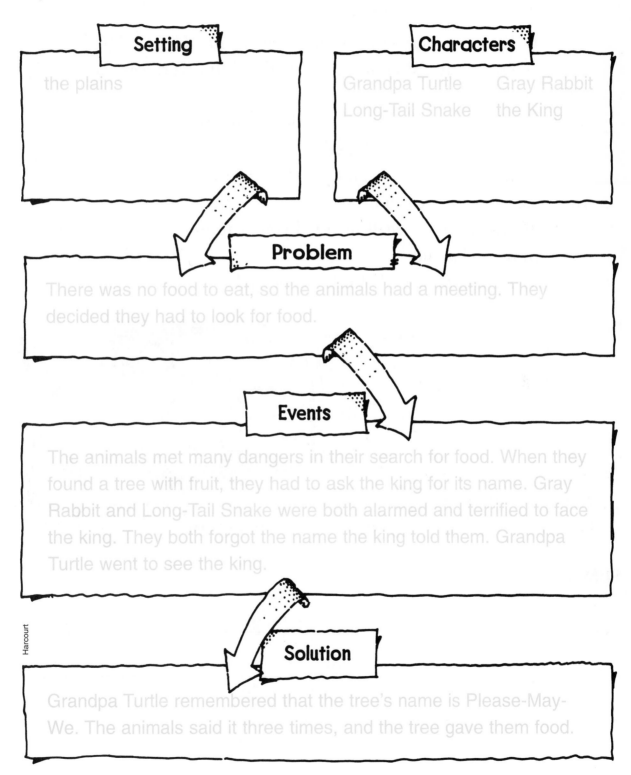

Setting

the plains

Characters

Grandpa Turtle   Gray Rabbit
Long-Tail Snake   the King

Problem

There was no food to eat, so the animals had a meeting. They decided they had to look for food.

Events

The animals met many dangers in their search for food. When they found a tree with fruit, they had to ask the king for its name. Gray Rabbit and Long-Tail Snake were both alarmed and terrified to face the king. They both forgot the name the king told them. Grandpa Turtle went to see the king.

Solution

Grandpa Turtle remembered that the tree's name is Please-May-We. The animals said it three times, and the tree gave them food.

Harcourt

Summarize

Read the story. Then write a summary of the story.

Little Turtle was very sad. His best friend, Little Gray Rabbit, was going to move away. "Who will I play with?" Little Turtle asked. "What will I do without my best friend?"

"I will wish on the first star every night that you are happy and having fun," Little Gray Rabbit said.

"I will make the same wish for you," Little Turtle said. "I will send you e-mail and pictures, too."

"I will answer your e-mail and send you pictures of my new home," Little Gray Rabbit said.

"This is going to be fun!" Little Turtle said.

SUMMARY

Possible response: Little Gray Rabbit was moving away. He and

Little Turtle decided to keep in touch by e-mail.

Harcourt

Fluency Builder

latch	just	below
dusk	because	sorrow
cunning	lived	shadow
embraced	wanted	own
tender	said	tomorrow
brittle	dark	narrow
delighted		snow

1. Just below a mountain / lived a farmer / and his wife.

2. Sorrow / hung over them / like a dark shadow / because they wanted / a baby / of their own.

3. "I see / a baby / on the top / of the mountain," / said Willow / as she gazed / out the window.

4. The farmer / embraced Willow / and lifted / the latch.

5. "Expect me / tomorrow / at dusk," / he said.

6. The farmer / had to pull himself / up narrow cliffs / of brittle, / frozen snow.

7. When the farmer / got home, / he showed Willow / a baby girl, / Snowflake, / with tender / little toes, / and Willow was / delighted.

8. Many years later, / a cunning fellow / wanted to trick Snowflake, / but the snow / saved her.

The Snow Baby

Read the story, and circle all the long *o* words.

Joe said, "Sue, come with me! I will show you something."

"What is it?" asked Sue.

Joe said, "Come and you will know." They went to the dock and got into Joe's rowboat. The boat floated on the lake.

When they got to the far side of the lake, Joe said, "Follow me." He walked on tiptoes. Then Sue spotted a little doe in the grass! Joe smiled and said, "I will call her Snow."

Now write the long *o* word that completes each sentence.

1. Joe wants to _____ something to Sue.

2. Sue wants to _____ what it is.

3. Joe takes Sue in his _____.

4. Joe tells Sue to _____ him.

5. Joe walks on _____.

6. Sue sees a _____ that Joe

names _____.

Harcourt

The Snow Baby

Complete the flowchart with words from the box to tell about "The Snow Baby."

wink	window	save	baby	mountain

The farmer's wife gazes out the

___window___.

She sees a

___baby___

at the top of the

___mountain___.

The farmer goes to

___save___

the baby.

In the

___wink___

of an eye, she is all grown up.

Answer these questions to tell what happens in the rest of the story.

1. Why does Snowflake go with the cunning fellow?

He pretends to be gentle and kind.

2. Why does Snowflake get out of the coach?

The fellow loses his temper and yells at the horses.

3. How does she get home?

The snow shows her the way back to her parents.

Harcourt

Compare and Contrast

Read the story. Think about how it is like "The Snow Baby" and how it is different. Complete the sentences to compare and contrast this story with "The Snow Baby."

The Apple Baby

One day a farmer and his wife were picking apples. Then the farmer found something in the branches of the apple tree. It was a little baby girl. Her cheeks were as red and round as apples. The farmer and his wife had been wanting a baby of their own. They called her Little Apple. They were a very happy family.

COMPARE

1. The man in both stories is a _____ farmer _____.

2. The man and his wife find a _____ baby *or* baby girl _____.

CONTRAST

3. Snowflake is found in _____ the snow _____.

4. Little Apple is found in _____ a tree *or* an apple tree _____.

Harcourt

Fluency Builder

wits	**family**	**so**
wailing	**into**	**tiny**
advice	**some**	**over**
dreadful	**talk**	**she**
faring	**look**	**kind**
farewell	**lost**	**he**
		we
		told

1. The Gold family / thinks their house / is so tiny / that they have / no room / to move.

2. They ask / Ms. Post, / the wisest person / in town, / for some advice.

3. Ms. Post / comes over / to talk about / the family's problem.

4. She tells them / to bring the hens / into the house, / and they do.

5. Brian Gold / is wailing / because / he just stepped on / an egg / and broke it.

6. "Look at / the kind of mess / we are in now," / says Mr. Gold / to Ms. Post.

7. Ms. Post / tells him / to bring the goats / and cows / into the house.

8. "This will be / dreadful, / but we will do / what we're told," / says Mr. Gold.

9. Ms. Post / asks how / the Golds are faring. / "We have lost / our wits," / says Mr. Gold.

10. "Take the animals / outside again," / says Ms. Post. / "Farewell."

Good Advice

Write the word that answers each riddle.

1. First, I lose it. Next, I look
for it. Now, I ____ it.

What am I? _____find_____
  fend   fond   find

2. I am yellowish. I cost a lot.

What am I? _____gold_____
  gold   good   grind

3. I mean "not mean."

What am I? _____kind_____
  kid   kind   cold

4. I stand for the person speaking.

What am I? _____me_____
  mind   me   mow

5. I mean "not hot."

What am I? _____cold_____
  cod   code   cold

6. I mean "you and I."

What am I? _____we_____
  we   woke   wind

7. You use your hands to do me.

What am I? _____hold_____
  hind   heel   hold

Harcourt

Name _____

Good Advice

These events are from "Good Advice." They are out of order. Put a number in front of each one to show the right order.

_____3_____ Father brings the goats and cows inside.

_____4_____ Father takes the animals outside.

_____1_____ Mrs. Gold tells the children to pick up their things.

_____2_____ Ms. Post tells Mr. Gold to bring the hens inside.

Now write each event in the order in which it happened. Put each one next to the correct number. Then add a sentence to tell what happened next.

1. Mrs. Gold tells the children to pick up their things.

   _____

2. Ms. Post tells Mr. Gold to bring the hens inside.

   _____

3. Father brings the goats and cows inside.

   _____

4. Father takes the animals outside.

   _____

5. Possible response: The family is happy because they think

   their house is bigger.

Harcourt

Author's Purpose

Name _____

Complete each sentence by writing the author's main purpose. Use a purpose from the box.

to entertain	to inform	to persuade	to give instructions

This book explains the sounds that whales make. It tells many facts about whales.

The author's purpose is ___to inform___

_____ .

The author of this book says that girls and boys need to read more and not watch so much TV.

The author's purpose is ___to persuade___

_____ .

This book tells how to make toys and games from things that most of us would throw away.

The author's purpose is ___to give___

___instructions_____ .

This book tells a story about a girl who finds a lost pup and wants to keep it for her own.

The author's purpose is ___to___

___entertain_____ .

Fluency Builder

glistened	could	would
county	everyone	Ty
galloped	horses	sky
clutched	start	crying
bid	began	by
auctioneer	enough	try
	knew	flying

1. Tyrone / worked hard / so he could get / a pony / called Blue Sky.

2. Everyone / in the county / came to see / the wild horses / at the sale.

3. Ty / was there / with his money / clutched / in his hand.

4. The auctioneer / called out / that it was time / to start / the sale.

5. When the bids / began, / Ty / felt like crying.

6. He didn't have / enough money / to get / Blue Sky, / but he / would try.

7. Everyone in town / knew how much / Ty wanted / that pony, / so no one / made a bid.

8. Blue Sky's / blue-black coat / glistened / in the sun.

9. As she galloped by, / her mane / was flying / in the wind.

10. Blue Sky / would never be happy / living on / a farm.

Auction Day

Fill in the oval in front of the sentence that best tells about the picture.

1 ◯ Ty looks at the winter sky.
   ⬭ Ty sees a butterfly.
   ◯ A butterfly flies in the sky.

2 ⬭ Pam flies the kite.
   ◯ Pam will fly the plane.
   ◯ Pam sees a fly in the sky.

3 ◯ My dog tries to fly!
   ⬭ My shy dog hides.
   ◯ My shy dog dries off.

4 ⬭ I am frying an egg.
   ◯ I am trying to crack an egg.
   ◯ I am spying on Dad.

5 ◯ The dog flies after the ball.
   ◯ The dog tries to eat.
   ⬭ The dog dries off.

6 ◯ Tim pets the shy pigs.
   ⬭ Tim sees pigs in the pig sty.
   ◯ Tim tries to dry the pigs.

7 ◯ Jill's plane is trying to land on the ground.
   ◯ Jill sees a butterfly on the plane.
   ⬭ Jill waves good-bye from the plane.

Harcourt

Auction Day

Complete the flowchart with words from the box to tell what happened in "Auction Day."

bank	money	borrows
neighbors	farm	pony

Ty spies a

_____pony_____

in the pen of wild horses.

➡

Ty goes to the

_____bank_____

to see how much

_____money_____

he has there.

➡

The man at the bank asks if a wild pony would be good on a

_____farm_____.

Ty asks his

_____neighbors_____

for work.

➡

Ty

_____borrows_____

a horse so he can get his six dollars from the bank.

➡

Ty buys Blue Sky.

Answer these questions to tell about the rest of the story.

Possible responses are given.

1. What happens at the auction? No one else bids on the pony.

_____

2. How does the story end? Ty frees the pony.

_____

3. How do you think Ty feels at the end of the story? He feels happy and

proud that Blue Sky is free, but he also feels sad because he misses her.

Harcourt

Fact and Opinion

Read these sentences about "Auction Day."
Write *Fact* or *Opinion* for each sentence.

1. Ty had six dollars in the bank. _____ Fact

2. Ty swept the floor in the store. _____ Fact

3. I think Ty was a good worker. _____ Opinion

4. Ty bid on Blue Sky at the auction. _____ Fact

5. I believe Blue Sky needed to be free. _____ Opinion

6. In my opinion, Ty did the right thing. _____ Opinion

Harcourt

Fluency Builder

ranchers	along	George
profit	all	Gemson
tending	must	range
corral	good	judge
stray	work	nudge
market	ready	gently
	over	gentle

1. Howdy, / partner! / Glad to have you / riding along / on this cattle drive.

2. My name / is George Gemson, / but you / can call me / Cookie.

3. My job / is to cook / for all you cowhands / on the range.

4. I'm sure / the trail boss / is a fair judge / of skill, / so you / must be good / with horses.

5. Tending cattle / is hard work.

6. Keep / an eye out / for stray cows.

7. These ranchers / want their cattle herds / to bring / a good price / in the market.

8. They want to / make money / —a profit.

9. I won't / nudge you gently / to wake you up / when breakfast / is ready.

10. You go on over / to the corral / and pick out / a gentle horse.

Harcourt

Name _____

A Cookie for the Cowboys

Write the word that answers each riddle.

1. I begin like *gem*. You go to me at school. What am I?

_____
gum   gym   gem

2. I end like *cage*. I mean "very, very big." What am I?

_____
huge   hug   hedge

3. I am very sweet to eat. I end like *edge*. What am I?

_____
flag   wedge   fudge

4. I am something you can play. I begin like *goat*.

What am I? _____
game   giant   germ

5. I am an animal. I begin like *gerbil*. What am I?

_____
gorilla   giraffe   ginger

6. Plants grow in me. I begin like *go*.

What am I? _____
gently   gerbil   garden

7. I end like *judge*. I can go over a river.

What am I? _____
badge   bridge   brag

Harcourt

A Cookie for the Cowboys

Think about the selection "A Cookie for the Cowboys." Write four things you learned from the selection.
Possible responses are given.

1. A cowboy rides a horse all day on a cattle drive.

_____

2. A cowboy's job is to keep the cattle together and moving slowly

toward the market.

3. The cows eat and grow fat on the way to the market.

_____

4. The chuck wagon is where the cook stores all the food and the trail

boss stores his papers and maps.

Write an answer to the question.

5. Would you like to go on a cattle drive? Why or why not?

Responses will vary.

_____

_____

Harcourt

Main Idea and Details

Read this passage from "A Cookie for the Cowboys."
Write answers to the questions.

Tending cattle is hard work. You'll be riding a horse all day long. You'll be very dirty. You'll eat dust.

1. Which sentence from this passage tells the main idea?

Tending cattle is hard work. _____

_____

2. Write three details from the passage that tell more about the main idea.

You'll be riding a horse all day long. _____

You'll be very dirty. _____

You'll eat dust. _____

_____

Harcourt

Fluency Builder

stagecoach	baked	downright
miner	started	overnight
nuggets	named	daylight
skillet	around	twilight
settle	found	moonlight
boom town	first	starlight
landmark		fright

1. My grandmother, / Mrs. Emma Lee Main / of High Mount, Tennessee, / was / downright clever.

2. She baked pies / and gave us / wild rides / in her wagon.

3. Then / Grandmama / went out West / and started / a stagecoach business.

4. Grandmama / busted broncos / by giving them / delicious apple pies / in a skillet.

5. Overnight, / Mrs. Emma Lee Main / became a miner / and got a mule / named Fred.

6. She dug / in the daylight, / twilight, / moonlight, / and starlight.

7. The pile of dirt / got so high, / it became a landmark / in the town of Pike.

8. People came / from miles around / to settle there, / and Pike became / a boom town.

9. Grandmama / found two gold nuggets / the very first day.

10. Next, / Grandmama became / a sheriff, / and what a fright / she gave / those wild cowhands!

Harcourt

How Grandmama Tamed the West

Write the word that answers each riddle.

1. I can go after *flash* or *star*. What am I? _____

                                                   sight   light   bright

2. I come at the end of the day. What am I? _____

                                                  night   sigh   nine

3. I can go up in the sky. What am I? _____

                            butterfly   highway   nightgown

4. I am the hand that isn't on your left.

What am I? _____

                          high   hide   right

5. I can fly. You hold on to me with a string.

What am I? _____

                          pie   kite   fight

6. We are little bugs. What are we? _____

                              flight   flies   fries

7. I flash in the sky. What am I? _____

                          trying   tight   lightning

Circle and write the word that best completes each sentence.

8. Ben and Ann were driving on the _____.

                          highway   light   highlight

9. There was _____ all around them.

                 light   lightning   lighthouse

10. When the car broke down, Ann used a _____.

                     nightlight   flashlight   flashbulb

Harcourt

Name

How Grandmama Tamed the West

Answer the questions to tell about "How Grandmama Tamed the West."

What did Grandmama bake?	Where does Grandmama go when she finds life in High Mount too tame?	The stagecoach left Mud Flats on Saturday. When did it get to Dry Gulch?
cakes and pies	out West	Friday, the day before it left

What do Grandmama and her mule set off to do?	What did they call the pile of dirt that Grandmama dug?	What did Grandmama do after she left the mining business?
dig for gold	Pike's Peak	became a sheriff

Why do so many towns have a street called Main Street?

named for Grandmama,

Mrs. Emma Lee Main

Name _____

Fact and Opinion

Read these sentences about "How Grandmama Tamed the West."
Write *Fact* or *Opinion* for each sentence.

1. Grandmama baked delightful pies. ____Opinion____

2. She started a stagecoach business. ____Fact____

3. Grandmama got a mule named Rube. ____Fact____

4. She was the best miner of them all. ____Opinion____

5. It's boring when things get quiet. ____Opinion____

6. Many towns have a Main Street. ____Fact____

Harcourt

Fluency Builder

trading	off	family
schooner	inside	party
harvest	left	everybody
machete	their	memory
pulp	made	hurried
bargain		tiny
support		snowy
		safely

1. It's harvest time, / and my family / is going to have / a party.

2. "Everybody / bring a memory-maker," / said Dad / as he hurried off / to work.

3. On Saturday, / I went / to the trading market.

4. I was looking for / a memory-maker.

5. At last, / I found / a tiny / plastic / sailing schooner / that was / a bargain.

6. I glued / the ship / inside the jar lid / and put glitter / and water / in the jar.

7. At the party / I said, / "I'm thankful / that Dad's grandma / and grandpa / left their cold / and snowy home / and sailed safely / to Galveston Island."

8. Dad / got his machete / and cut / the bananas.

9. Mom and I / helped support / the bunch / as Dad / cut the stem.

10. We mashed / the bananas / to a pulp / and made / pans of banana muffins.

Harvest Time

Complete the story with words from the birthday cake.

cookies ready
party really
Chief hungry
cuddly puppy

"I am _____ready_____ for Timmy's birthday

_____party_____, Dad," said Jimmy. "Can we go now?"

"Yes," said Dad.

There was a lot of food at the party. "It's a good thing I'm

_____hungry_____," said Jimmy. "I can eat cake

and _____cookies_____!"

Timmy got a surprise gift from Mom and Dad. It was a

_____puppy_____! It was soft and _____cuddly_____.

"Thank you," said Timmy. "I am _____really_____ happy.

I will name my dog _____Chief_____. This is a happy birthday
for me!"

Harvest Time

Write the following events in the order in which they happened in the story. Then write what happened at the end of the story.

Lizzie's family cut bananas from a tree.

Lizzie found a memory-maker at the market.

Lizzie's family took bananas to the neighbors.

Lizzie's parents showed her their memory-makers.

1. Lizzie found a memory-maker at the market.

_____

2. Lizzie's parents showed her their memory-makers.

_____

3. Lizzie's family cut bananas from a tree.

_____

4. Lizzie's family took bananas to the neighbors.

_____

5. Possible responses: The family made banana milkshakes, banana ice pops, and banana muffins; they had fun cooking and eating banana treats.

Compare and Contrast

Complete the sentences to compare and contrast the stories "Cocoa Ice" and "Harvest Time." Use words from the box.

Texas   girls   two   treats

COMPARE

1. The main characters are _____ girls _____ .

2. Families in both stories make _____ treats _____ .

CONTRAST

3. "Cocoa Ice" has _____ two _____ parts.

4. "Harvest Time" is set in _____ Texas _____ .

Harcourt

Fluency Builder

congratulations	what's	Boyd
value	your	point
amount	right	enjoy
receive	away	Roy
combinations	knows	toy
choices	birthday	coins
	year	
	her	

1. "A penny saved / is a penny earned" / is a wise saying.

2. What's the point / of saving / your money?

3. Why not / spend it / right away / and enjoy it / now?

4. The Boyd family / knows why.

5. Each year, / Roy Boyd / receives money / for his birthday, / and he spends it / on a toy / right away.

6. This year, / Roy / will save / his birthday money / until he knows / all his choices.

7. Mrs. Boyd / pays with / combinations of coins / when she / rides the bus.

8. Mrs. Boyd / saves her coins / so she has / the right amount.

9. Mr. Boyd / knows the value / of a dollar, / and the Boyds / also / save their money / in the bank.

10. If you can save / what you earn, / congratulations!

Penny Savers

Read each word and draw a picture for it. Pictures will vary.

1. boys

2. toys

3. coins

4. soil

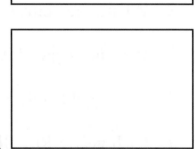

5. oyster

6. coiled

Write a story, using at least four of the words from above. Circle the words.

Stories will vary but should include at least four words from above. _____

_____

_____

_____

_____

_____

Harcourt

Penny Savers

Read each sentence. Write what happens next in the story.
Possible responses are given.

---

1. Roy spends all of his birthday money.

→

2. He doesn't have enough money to buy a toy car he wants.

---

3. Joy doesn't have enough money to buy skates.

→

4. Joy will save her money and earn some more to get enough to buy the skates.

---

5. Mrs. Boyd needs coins for the bus.

→

6. She saves the coins she gets as change to use when she wants to ride the bus.

---

7. Mr. Boyd wants to have money for a rainy day.

→

8. Mr. Boyd saves money in the bank.

Harcourt

Main Idea and Details

Read the paragraph. Write a sentence that states the main idea.

Some coin collectors look for old coins. Others collect coins from other lands. Some like coins with pictures based on a theme, such as animals, plants, or ships.

Main Idea: Possible response: Coin collectors can have different ideas about what kinds of coins to collect.

Fluency Builder

signal	again	book
celebrations	because	good
choosy	plant	cook
average	down	took
tracks	first	soon
admiring	friend	blooms
	little	
	everywhere	

1. I am going to / write in this book / each day / until / my sister Sue / is home again.

2. April 6: / Today was / a good day / because / we worked / in the garden. / I will plant / carrot seeds.

3. April 9: / Today, / I walked down / every row / of fruit trees, / admiring / the blossoms.

4. Remember when / you helped me / bake my first / apple pie, / and I felt like / a real cook?

5. April 13: / Today / was / an average day.

6. At the beach, / I was choosy / about / which rocks / I took home / for you.

7. In the sand, / I saw tracks / of our friend / the fox / and some baby foxes.

8. April 22: / Today, / I made a wish / on a rainbow, / and Mom said / she had / a feeling / it would come true / soon.

9. April 22: / The garden / must have heard / a signal / at night.

10. This morning, / there were leaves / and blooms / and little celebrations / everywhere.

Harcourt

Book of Days

Read the story. Circle the words that have the same vowel sounds as in _book_ or _food_.

Roody the Rooster

One afternoon, Roody the rooster went home to roost. He found an egg in his nook in the coop!

"Cock-a-doodle-doo!" he said. "Why is an egg in my nook? I feel foolish, but I will sit on the egg."

Just then the egg shook. Roody hopped off, and the egg cracked open. Roody saw a webbed foot.

"That's not a chicken's foot," said Roody. Soon a baby goose came out! "Oh, no!" said Roody. "Goosy the goose laid an egg in the chicken coop!"

Now write one of the words you circled to complete each sentence.

1. Roody is a _____ rooster _____.

2. He lives in a chicken _____ coop _____.

3. Roody finds an egg in his _____ nook _____.

4. Roody feels _____ foolish _____ sitting on the egg.

5. A webbed _____ foot _____ comes out.

6. Roody sees a baby _____ goose _____.

Harcourt

Book of Days

Complete the flowchart with words from the box to tell what happened in the first part of "Book of Days."

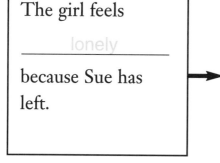

remember	date	myself
rainbow	charge	lonely

The girl feels

___lonely___

because Sue has left.

→

The girl writes the

___date___

at the top of every page in her book!

→

The girl puts herself in

___charge___

of Sue's flower box.

Sue had said that a

___rainbow___

of flowers would grow in the flower box.

→

One day the girl wrote, "Today I put

___myself___

in charge of the fruit trees."

→

The girl can

___remember___

picking apples with Sue.

Answer these questions to tell what happened during the rest of the story.

1. What does the girl see by the river? What does this mean to her? Possible response: She sees fox tracks. This means spring is really here.

2. What happens after the rain stops? Possible response: The little sister sees a rainbow and makes a wish.

3. What happens at the end of the story? Possible responses: The garden blooms. Sue comes home. The family has a big celebration.

Harcourt

Summarize

Read the paragraph. Write a sentence to summarize the paragraph.

Have you ever seen a real coyote in the wild? Coyotes are found in almost every state of the United States. Some live close to cities and towns. Even if coyotes live nearby, you might not see one. Coyotes hunt mostly at night. They try to stay away from people, and they can run very fast.

SUMMARY:

Possible response: Coyotes live in many places, but it is hard to see them. _____

_____

_____

Harcourt

Fluency Builder

windmill	asked	Cyrus
cherished	could	city
furrows	use	cement
ample	made	space
shunned	there's	Cecil
growth	through	cellar
	flower(s)	
	beautiful	

1. Cyrus / asked his dad / if he / could have a pet, / but the rule / was no dogs / in the building.

2. "You can use / the backyard / to make a garden / for city birds / that need help," / said Dad.

3. "Our backyard / is made of cement, / and there's no space / for a garden / out there!" / said Cy.

4. Cy / looked through bird books / and hoped / the visitors / would be hummingbirds.

5. "Our little garden / has ample space / for such tiny birds," / said Dad.

6. Mrs. Cecil / gave Cy / old pots / from her cellar.

7. Cy dug / little furrows / in the dirt, / planted the seeds / for red flowers, / and watched for / signs of growth.

8. At first, / the hummingbirds / shunned / his beautiful garden.

9. One day, / he saw / a hummingbird / with its wings going / like little windmills.

10. Cy cherished / the time he spent / with his new pets.

The Hummingbird Garden

Read each word, and think about the sound *c* stands for. Write it in the correct column.

| mice | cent | cake | icy | cucumber | center | cold | cow |

city

cat

mice	_cake_
cent	_cucumber_
icy	_cold_
center	_cow_

Write four sentences. In each sentence, use one word from each column above. Responses will vary.

1. _____

2. _____

3. _____

4. _____

Harcourt

Name _____

The Hummingbird Garden

These events are from "The Hummingbird Garden." They are out of order. Put a number in front of each one to show the right order.

_____3_____ Cy filled the bird feeder and waited for hummingbirds.

_____1_____ Cy said, "I want our visitors to be hummingbirds."

_____4_____ Summer turned to fall.

_____2_____ Cy planted flower seeds in the garden.

Now write each event from above where it belongs in the story.

Cy asked his dad if he could have a pet.

Cy's dad told him he should make a garden for city birds.

Cy looked at bird books.

Cy said, "I want our visitors to be hummingbirds."

Cy decided that hummingbirds would like red and pink flowers.

Cy planted flower seeds in the garden.

Cy filled the bird feeder and waited for hummingbirds.

Birds came to the bird feeder all summer long.

Summer turned to fall.

The hummingbirds flew south for the winter.

Cause and Effect

Write a cause or an effect from the box to complete each sentence.

CAUSES	EFFECTS
hummingbirds drink sweet water	Cy planted red flowers
his backyard was made of cement	the hummingbirds did not return

1. Cy planted a garden in pots because _____

_____ his backyard was made of cement _____ .

2. Hummingbirds like red and pink flowers, so _____

_____ Cy planted red flowers _____ .

3. Cy filled the feeder with sweet water because _____

_____ hummingbirds drink sweet water _____ .

4. Summer turned to fall. As a result, _____

_____ the hummingbirds did not return _____ .

Harcourt

Fluency Builder

magma	along	began
edges	ago	near
range	rock	very
epicenter	hard	caused
coast	started	caught
peak	beautiful	awesome
	ground	saw

1. The chain of mountains / called the Cascade Range / runs along / the west coast / of North America.

2. The mountains / in this range / are beautiful.

3. These peaks / were formed / long ago / by volcanoes.

4. Deep in the center / of our planet / is hot melted rock / called magma.

5. On top of it / float plates / of hard rock / that form / the planet's crust.

6. In 1980 / the plates / under the Cascade Range / started to shift.

7. The edges / of the plates / pushed up the magma / and caused / Mount St. Helens to bulge.

8. On Sunday, / May 18, / 1980, / Mount St. Helens / caught the early rays / of the sun, / and then / the ground began / to shake.

9. The epicenter / of the quake / was / very near / Mount St. Helens.

10. When the big blasts stopped, / the people saw / an awesome sight.

Name _____

Fill in the oval in front of the sentence that tells about the picture.

1 ◯ Paul saw a fawn.
⬭ Paul does a jigsaw puzzle.
◯ Paul puzzles over the hawk.

2 ◯ The girl has a straw hat.
⬭ The girl uses a straw to drink.
◯ The girl sees straw on the lawn.

3 ⬭ The baby is crawling.
◯ The baby is crying.
◯ The baby caught a ball.

4 ◯ She draws a lion.
◯ She drinks a lemonade.
⬭ She does her laundry.

5 ⬭ His daughter saw a fawn.
◯ His daughter pointed to a hawk.
◯ His daughter crawled on the lawn.

6 ⬭ Paws gives me a paw.
◯ Paws plays ball on the lawn.
◯ Paws saw a hawk.

A Mountain Blows Its Top

Fill in the first two columns of the K-W-L chart before you read "A Mountain Blows Its Top." Fill in the last column after you finish reading.

K	W	L
What I Know	**What I Want to Know**	**What I Learned**
Responses will vary.		

This is the most interesting fact I learned:

Responses will vary.

_____

_____

_____

Harcourt

Locate Information

This is a nonfiction book. It has a table of contents, a glossary, and an index.

Write the answer to each question.

1. What it the title of this book?

Mount St. Helens

2. Where would you look to find out what a *crater* is?

glossary

3. Where would you look to find out the names of the chapters in the book?

table of contents

4. Where would you look to find out what pages have information about Yakima, Washington?

index

5. Where would you look to find out what page Chapter 3 begins on?

table of contents

Harcourt

Fluency Builder

eventually	around	would
converse	just	begin
continent	pulled	wrapping
sphere	watched	wrist
universe	fell	knew
homeward	our	wren
	between	knitted

1. "Good night, Will," / said Mom, / wrapping her cool hand / around my wrist.

2. Mom knew / that my dreams / could take me places.

3. "I might / just go / far out / into the universe, / Mom," / I said.

4. "We can / converse about it / in the morning," / she said, / as she pulled up / my knitted blanket.

5. My night-light / is a blue-and-green sphere / that glows / as it twirls.

6. I watched it / for a while, / and eventually / I fell asleep.

7. I soared up / and followed my friend / the wren / higher and higher.

8. Soon / I could see / our country / between two big seas.

9. Our country / is as wide / as the whole continent, / and the world / is a blue-and-green sphere.

10. As morning came, / I knew / we would have to begin / our long flight / homeward.

The Place in Space

Read the story. Circle the words that begin like _knot_ or _write_.

Wrangle couldn't find his wristwatch. "I don't know where
it is. I had it when I was writing letters, wrangling cattle, and
wrestling with the dogs." He knelt down and looked under
his bed. He found kneepads. He turned the knob to his closet
door. He found a knapsack and some knickers. He looked in
the kitchen and saw a knife. Then he looked out the window.
A wren was sitting in the tree. It had something shiny.
"There's my wristwatch!" said Wrangle.

Now answer each question with a word you circled.

1. What couldn't Wrangle find? _____wristwatch_____

2. What did Wrangle find under the bed? _____kneepads_____

3. What did Wrangle turn? _____knob_____

4. What did he find in the closet? ___a knapsack and some knickers___

5. What was in the tree? _____wren_____

6. What did it have? _____wristwatch_____

Harcourt

The Place in Space

Complete the sentences to tell about the story. Possible responses are given.

1. Will's mom wonders where Will will go in his dreams
_____.

2. Will goes to sleep. First, he sees his city from a mountaintop
_____.

3. In the sky, he sees a wren circling and calling to him
_____.

4. He flies up high over the clouds
_____.

5. Will and the wren see his state, his country, and then the
whole world _____.

6. Will's mom wakes Will up, and Will tells her about his dream; hears
a bird singing _____.

Cause and Effect

Write another effect for this cause. Use the words in the box.

CAUSE: Will and the wren flew higher and higher.

our   country

EFFECTS:

1. Will saw his entire state.

2. ___Possible response: Will saw our country.___

_____

Write another cause for this effect. Use the words in the box.

friends   together

EFFECT: Will and the wren were happy.

CAUSES:

3. Our planet looked beautiful.

4. ___Possible response: The two friends were together.___

_____

Harcourt

Fluency Builder

force   one   atmosphere
nucleus   from   enough
loops   like   trough
solar wind   tail   rough
particles   that's
fluorescent   little
because   left
behind   ground

1. Comets / are one kind / of visitor / to our planet / from space.

2. A comet / is a ball / of frozen gases.

3. The gases / are the nucleus, / or center, / of the comet.

4. Around the nucleus / is a cloud / that looks like / a tail.

5. That's because / a force from the sun, / called solar wind, / blows the cloud / out behind the comet.

6. At night, / a comet glows / like a fluorescent light.

7. Comets / loop around the sun / in orbits, / and so do meteors.

8. Every day, / millions of little / rock-like meteors / enter our atmosphere / and get hot enough / to glow.

9. Most of them / are tiny particles / about the size / of a grain of sand.

10. A huge meteor / slammed into our planet / 50,000 years ago / and left a deep crater, / or trough, / with rough / rocky ground / all around it.

A Meteor Stopped Here

Follow the directions in the sentences below.

1. Ralph is an elephant. Color Ralph blue.
2. Put Ralph's autograph on the photograph of Ralph.
3. Put a hat on the gopher.
4. Draw the missing part of the telephone.
5. Color the dolphin green.

Harcourt

A Meteor Stopped Here

Answer these questions about comets and meteors.

1. What causes the cloud around a comet's nucleus to look like a tail?

Wind from the sun blows the cloud out behind the comet.

2. What causes a comet to glow?

It reflects the sun's light.

3. What causes a meteor to glow?

It gets very hot.

4. Why do people call small meteors *shooting stars?*

When little meteors enter Earth's atmosphere, they look like

falling stars.

5. What happened when a huge meteor fell from the sky 50,000 years ago?

A huge crater, or hole, was made in the ground.

6. What happened to that meteor?

The meteor was destroyed. It turned into gases, it melted, or

it split into small pieces.

Harcourt

Name _____

Locate Information

This nonfiction book has a table of contents, chapter headings, a glossary, and an index.

Write the answer to each question.

1. Who is the author of *All About Meteors?* _____

   _____ Lucy Robbins _____

2. Where can you look to find out what page Chapter 5 begins on? _____

   _____ table of contents _____

3. Where can you look to find out what pages have information about

   Arizona? _____ index _____

4. Where can you look to find out what the sections of Chapter 2 tell about?

   _____ chapter headings _____

5. Where can you look to find the meaning of *trough*? _____

   _____ glossary _____